Government Economic Report

Government Economic Report

An Intelligence Officer's Viewpoint

By
Mohammed M. Hunafa

E-BookTime, LLC
Montgomery, Alabama

Government Economic Report
An Intelligence Officer's Viewpoint

ISBN: 978-1-60862-389-1

First Edition
Published April 2012
E-BookTime, LLC
6598 Pumpkin Road
Montgomery, AL 36108
www.e-booktime.com

Contents

Chapter 1

The Lay of the Land

In providing a true economic stimulus, one that objectifies the subject inherently and is not propitious in economic standings that in the past have not addressed the fluid approach to economics, I start off this book with a presupposition. The presupposition, as may be found throughout this chapter is one that insinuates is the basic explanation of what have been and are currently the placement in view of world economics which is relative for America. I would like to state at the outset to this thesis and especially here in the first chapter that the "Lay of the Land" chapter must be ubiquitous in explanation. Too many times intelligence officers fail to provide factors of which the reading public can make sense of. I wish to not be one of those officers. As I was thinking of what this thesis would mean to the general public as I began the research for it, I wished that it would be far better than most other thesis on the market covering this subject. I wished that it would be a fluid, easy to read diagram of the state of economics in the world today and a diagram that all readers could comprehend. I find as an intelligence officer that I have a duty and an obligation to the respected reader of such a great science to give precise and applicable estimates and calculations in economics in order to have done the job of reporting intelligence the best that is possible. Therefore, where other's thesis give you pages of filler that sometimes detract from an economic treatise, I give you truth and application of economics that really apply to the real world.

Having said that, I would like to start keeping the promise just made to you by jumping right into the telling of this story. In the beginning of this country's history, economy as it was in those days was only farm labor oriented. There were not a lot of extravagances that added to higher quality of life. The clothing was hand sewn or some form of archaic sewing. Food was grown from husbandry of farm animals. Transportation was meager. So what these words translated to a picturesque advantage provide us is that America was just where most industrializing nations of past and present were in their history. There are even some nations of the world yet to become industrialized nations. What can be said for America is that it had a promise in being able to industrialize that was more probable because many of the first Americans had come from an industrialized nation themselves and had that experience to guide them. Most were already experienced tradesmen. In terms of economics, by default America was prone to economically advance in the western hemisphere by itself. Not much need or opportunity existed to trade and barter with other nations. The country plied its path along in this way until the advent of the industrial revolution starting in the late 1800's and early 1900's. In this period America would seemingly transition overnight to become a land that at least in the northeastern region of the country would be dotted with major cities with the invention of the industrial plants and its newly designed assembly line. In the southeastern portion of the country there were many rural plantations that were the bedrock of the economy for that part of the country. So to better provide a picture of what this transition meant to the everyday American, their lives had become somewhat advanced to the lifestyles that they lived before and up to 1800. Now their lives were beginning to show promise through the job market but most still were not yet educated enough to make any contribution to the workplace advantageous enough that their employer might make the kind of input into the American economy that was sustainable. Then came the Great Depression of the 1920's.

The Great Depression was foremost the most devastating period of American history. Factories that had virtually blossomed overnight shut their doors. To those few that had found jobs in the factories after having left the farm after it failed as an instrument to keep pace with an ever escalating demand of the public economy they were out of work. The big industry that had come to America so quickly was gone. The industrial revolution was a transition in fact for America but it also was a period that took America off guard and one the American landscape was not truly ready for. The industrial revolution of course was the answer to a quick upsurge in economic spending by the private sector that was the way private business answered the call for an ever demanding public to be provided with production as a country than could have been. The industrial revolution really was a pace too fast and too much for the country. We were not really prepared to take on the responsibility that went along with being an industrial power and perhaps are not yet there today. So virtually, and I mean virtually, the industrial revolution was gone as fast as it had come. Some might say that that is not so, America has done wonderfully as an industrial nation. I beg to differ. The reality that the products of the period went out of demand very well from that period to today says that we are not industrialist. We in today's time are a service oriented nation, not industrial. That is a fact, after we passed through our try at being industrialists, we settled on service. This is because of the hard facts of reality that the economist where he or she is concerned with business does not have the management capability to really sustain the profiting that is foremost for businesses in an industrializing nation. We go to the best business schools and yet the fact still permeates straight through our seeming know how to show us the business we set out to show profits for three out of five times will close its doors in five years. The job of tackling the intangibles of economic business are just too big for us at this time. Who knows if we will ever be really great at the job of managing an economic concern.

Also I would like to introduce another point as to why we regressed in the fact of what has become the doing what we are good at (service industry oriented jobs) and were we fell short of (industrializing a nation) during the period. From the very beginning we always knew that the world was a place of limited resources and that we had to operate sparingly in the use of those resources if we were to make them last well into our future. As long as we stayed pre-era industrialists we did quite well, but it was the advent of the 20th century when we knew that scaling back in the use of certain resources was in need if they were to last us. So right about 1945 at the end of World War II we got a wake up call from that period of spending that let us know that if we kept up our present behavior we would be out of resources by the 26th century. Another form of financing of the world economy was in need and along came the Desta program. The Desta program will be the discussion of later chapters. For now I would like to step back a moment and show what benefits occurred in America in a period I call the "times of challenge". With the beginning of the 20th century American leadership was in demand not so much for what it could do for us politically as it was to do for us economically. The fact is the pre 20th century economy was virtually no challenge (the period has just sprouted when saving resources became our priority). It was at this time the 20th century and beset by a failing industrializing attempt and other factors did this become the times of challenge. Leaders in this 20th century would have to be astute students of economy as well as other disciplines to provide America the leadership that could sustain America in a time of challenge. So marked the 20th century era leaders. Some of the most respected were Franklin Delano Roosevelt, Herbert Hoover, Harry Truman and Ronald Reagan. Each of these leaders had at his respective time as national leader the opportunity to show through his dynamic style approaches at leadership that carried the country during stressful times. These were the men of steel reserve that truly delivered to the people when they needed it most. Our second chapter is entitled "The Designers" and I hope you will be instructed in that chapter as I have intended this entire thesis to be.

Chapter 2

The Designers

The emphatic term "Designers" could very well have been a term like creator or inventor that could have been used to denote someone of original genius. I chose this word as I have an infinity that likes to connect words that compliment the word with that that is actually what type of work they produce. So here the design or plan of these great justifiers of American economy is suitable to impress the mind that they, the "Designers", are indeed of great import to American economic invention. Greats in American industry like Carnegie, Vanderbilt, Morgan and Rockefeller are just a few who had the right stuff to improve on what they started. Leaving in the end us all better than when they began. Others as was mentioned in chapter one of the political sphere are names like

Hoover, Roosevelt, Truman and Reagan. These were the leaders of the 20th century that in no other way only through the opportunity that the 20th century challenge produced had the ability to prove they were great indeed.

What makes a Designer? Who are those that flock around them? What do they really offer the world in which they live? The answer to the first question is reputation. In reputation they are proven mavericks of idea that preeminently pave a path and frontier in American economic advantage that of their periods was unheralded. They have the wherewithal to be comptrollers of the "big picture" in economic advancement. They understand macro and micro economics second naturedly and know as well the moves that make for sound economic principles, plans and policy.

In providing the answer to the second question, I say those who flock around "Designers" are those who know a wealth builder when they experience one. People from all walks of life. Whether rich or poor. White or black. Male or female. Child or adult. They are those that tailor themselves to the quips of every great "Designer". Working as instruments of innovation through the designers plan of a better economic tomorrow, the "Designers" do all that the people adore them for.

Thirdly, "Designers" offer to this one world, with its limited resources, a way to make the little resources we have appear to be much. They offer in times of strife the exacting embodiment of unparalleled prosperity other economists fail to resonate. For this thesis, in addition to the above set of definitions, a "Designer" in the 21st century is the central planner of economic objectives that are the center of a financial plan that takes the "Designers" creation and makes them happen. But here is something that you might find odd about a "Designer". They live antiquation. They are developers of ideas for a futuristic tomorrow. Their plans and activities center on premises of current eras of modernization that keep all inventions fresh and applicable no matter what age they represent. Also in this descriptive, today's "Designers" are on call not just here in America but throughout the world, applying great ideas on behalf of the American economy that in all ways does the best good for all concerned. They are on loan to a majority of the world's third world nations laying in innovative ideas of economic reformation that potentially can last years in the invested interest of the economies in which they work. On loan from

America to those foreign nations to assist them with their needs, they potentially are the glue that is holding economies the world over from a threatening insoluble ability to gain strength in the world today. So the "Designers" are all about the workings of pure economic stimulus. Stimulus that promotes the why of being central stage players to the American economy, European Union and World Bank in an association between the three to carry out a plan that will reformulate the idea of economic advantage the world over. America the E.U. and the World Bank came together shortly after World War II and formed a alliance that was about economic prosperity that would provide to fledgling nations funding that would wholly be devoted to establishing their economies. The program that developed from this alliance is a little known program outside of the alliance that is called "Desta". "Desta" works to make available through a lottery funds available that are used by these Third World Nations to bring their economies up to a level where they can compete economically with the rest of the world. It establishes a sound and beneficial base of capital from which the respective nation can began to alter its state of existence for the better. Chapter 3 will discuss the "Desta" program.

Chapter 3

The Desta Program

It has been a fact of history that in the post World War II era, America and very much the rest of the world had become ever more aware that the economies the world had proffered by up until the war were growing more and more straightened. The surge in spending economies were engaging in like paying for wars and nation building had placed them in positions of dismal prospect for survival. If major activities in spending were not given a new orientation depletion of the economic resources of most countries would be eminent. For those countries like America, Russia, Britain, Japan, Canada and China the end of World War II was a wake up call. New inventions in economic diversity in America became the new thinking and the selling off of major infrastructures was the extenuation of a little known funding program called Desta. Desta in America came about by a trend in this country that envisioned a Third World funding program that provided that America in essence would fund certain eco-works programs of smaller less established countries and in return reap the utilitarian rewards from the program when countries made good on provisions from initial funding. These countries would take the Desta funding, invest it in their own eco-works programs, build their infrastructure and commercial business areas of enterprise and in form when funding had to be repaid give back to America what had been provided plus a percentage of that country's GDP at a discount. This program was a brilliant stroke of genius for America because as the time had been reached where alternative economic stimulus had to be introduced, America could both help stabilize other economies and save her own. Throughout Europe in institutions like the World Bank and European Union, Desta had been practiced as late as 1950. As America became aware of the benefits of Desta it made good economic sense to start this type of program as a benefit to her own economy. Desta as a singular funding program that would reap the needed upgrade to America's economic system was the program of the ages. It was America's number one source for earning dividends that would have returns and mobilize its own economy in ways that had previously not been accomplished. The funding approach of Desta was the American economy in essence. By an ingenious method of lottery, America would pool together the names of competitor nations and draw from that lottery one to the last competing nations in successive order funding in increments that had more funding being provided to the top most lottery winner and lesser amounts down the line until all nations had received the fair share funding or the funding source ran out. The Desta program essentially provisioned the American economy with four safeguards to sustain the economy that would perpetuate well into the future. The four areas safe-netted by Desta were 1) use of other nations funds that would be paid back to America in many forms for having provided Desta funding. 2) That a new economic oriented set of corporations would spot the American landscape that would come into being on loans the government made to private commercial business with money from Desta that essentially would earn the government more revenues. The Desta program would help in all fashion. There would be a realization that inflationary aspects of the program were proofed against such reality and the American economy could then use excess funds of its own determination to stabilize the American economy. 3) In reverse to the facet just mentioned the long time program of subsidy that the American government had provided to businesses doing business in America instead of overseas could now be part of businesses own program. Subsidy would be paid back to the government in the form of the loans repayment that corporations would have to make back to the government. 4) This point is in conjunction to the E.U. and World Bank. America would receive special subsidies for being a partner in the world funding program they participated in with the E.U. and World Bank just for funding partnership in Desta to Third World countries.

There are not all rosy prospects for Desta. In all it does to promote eco-works and commercial business in the American mega firms like Skycom and Intercon. American firms who are a result of Desta. It does not cover all of the commercial market. There is much that because of the special funding restraints on provisional funds Desta can provide many areas of the economy are at present limited. In order for those other areas to not become the reasons that perhaps even with Desta whole economies destabilize, America and her Desta partners must rethink Desta. As we move into the future and there becomes an ever more demanding framework of diversity to assure economic markets flourish in all areas in all economies will have to be addressed. As I said Desta at present does not do all. Could other programs be created to compliment Desta? Perhaps, but the unique thing to do is not to make too many changes to what already works and the part that doesn't work well new thinking will have to address those areas. For right now Desta is good enough but surely in the next 50 + years the Desta program will have to be revised to keep pace with the demands of all economies to seek out renewable psychologies where people do not realize that advancements are indeed not being made. It should be remembered, in the demanding world we live in today, stagnation and decay are next to death of the world economy.

Chapter 4

Courtesy Acquittal Limit

In America through the Desta program to Third World developing nations a thing called the "Courtesy Acquittal Limit" is in play. Here is how it is applied. America through it's "Designers" on loan to Third World nations fund those countries with the understanding by both parties that the funds are a courtesy from America to the respective nation. Essentially a gift from the United States to foster prosperity. The term "acquittal" is the resonation that both sides experience mutuality to the cost. This mutuality is prevalent because neither America or the respective country is really in a suffered position in the exchange of these funds. America doesn't suffer because in the first place these funds set aside for Desta are not originally part of the framework capital that America uses to support her own economy. Simply these funds are outside of the budget America sets aside for her economic needs. In respect to the receiving nation, they suffer none because without this funding they would not have been able to address certain concerns of their economy. They only stand to gain in this venture. Having avoided unproductivity by taking part in the program is how suffering is not experienced. The only time the money is repaid is when the government experiences expansion. And the term limit as it is applied to the "Courtesy Acquittal Limit", means that there is an aggregate amount of funds that remains below a certain percentage of America's funds output that is not exceeded in order for no real tangible losses to be experienced. If the program funding goes bust America really losses nothing. Those were excess dollars it could have afforded to not be invested with hopes of a return so nothing is loss. The limit insures and financially so that built into the program is assuredness that it is on sound footing. This limit at different times can be raised or lowered in concert with inflation so the impact of the funding is always effective. Desta is made more secure hedge for improving America's wealth by the "Courtesy Acquittal Limit".

Chapter 5

Lottery of Competitors

"Lottery of Competitors" is a term that once broken down into its elemental words indicates that a lottery is set up by America. This approach insures that more funding than is allocatable is not needed to do the most good for the developing nations of the world. The lottery takes into account all needy nations from the Third World are added into the lottery. The most winning lottery competitor receive percentages of funds greater than amounts received by the number two nation and the third receiving nation receives even less than the second nation. The lottery approach was the only feasible way for the program to do a set amount of funding without being above the "Courtesy Acquittal Limit". Going above the limit means funds would have to come from other sources which are just not part of what America can afford. So the lottery is the next best thing. It is important to know why in lottery formula more money is paid to the most winning nation and lesser monies paid as may go down the list. Each country has to meet stipulations to show they are more deserving of the most funds than other nations so that they can receive the money and do the most good in their country. So they compete in kind. This program under the conditions facing struggling economies including the United States could not very well have been put together any other kind of way and still exist. In Desta is the one world mechanism to do anything in the way of nation building. Desta being the only vehicle to try anything in this advantage is doing good by what it does.

Chapter 6

Consumptive Era Estimates

"Consumptive Era Estimates" is a term that denotes by the first word that all the funding of the Desta program or for that matter any financing program using consumption as its base for funding is not greater than can be provided. In economic terms, it means that in an era were economies guard against over consumption from the little capital they have in reserve, spending must be budgeted that makes every dollar have the desired impact. It is understood that the world is a place where resources and capital are limited. Therefore in the interest of the Desta funding program, America has to allocate and then precipitate where all funding goes and if it will show returns on the original monies invested. There is the idea that these countries already are baseless as far as strong economies go. Therefore the specific projects must be just right and the knowledge must be sure that the returns from investing in the Desta program will be acquired in order for the program to work. Through the process of true consumption formulas, every dollar invested must have an estimated buy value. Every dollar when it has been valued with respect to what it can purchase in terms of production has to do more with what it acquires in product than it would if market value rates were above the dollar's valuation. Simply stated the dollar should buy what is needed with value for the dollar in purchasing power as if it was two or three dollars buying power more with respect to other currency and inflation. So this is the idea behind right formulated consumption of economic production. The term era as it implies must in the current era whenever that might be must do more with purchasing power than may have been in the past or future. That is easy enough stated but when it comes to the future that is the tricky part. You see in every successive age the dollar does more tomorrow than it did yesterday. That is easy enough understood. But here in this application with so much need for impact investment formulas of today needing to outstrip tomorrow until we get there the dollar must show proportionately better returns on its own value and that of future dollar values than at any time. That must be stair step approach to increasing the dollar's value today, tomorrow and at any time. So when tomorrow comes the approach to insuring above average formulation of purchasing power used to assure Desta must be the same incremental increased formula used tomorrow. And the word estimates in our scientific term denotes that these are all consumption estimates, era estimates and estimates in general that will imply a value on paper that can be arranged in any format to compete with inflation and what the dollar might buy when it is compared to other nations' currency. So this is the part of Desta that is very important in that through this facet all proportional numbers can be juggled until the program achieves in reality what it is outlined to do on paper.

Chapter 7

Complimentary Effect Increments

"Complimentary Effect Increments" is a term that denotes that above and beyond the lack of readily available resources any Third World nation may not possess to exact any eco-works programs, all funding is complimenting that fact after it is received and placed into a project. It also denotes that as far as effects there simply would be none without the American Desta program. Also it insinuates that effectively, a project that has been planned must work in theory, practice and in producing a return. Lastly the funding from Desta is provided through the lottery in sizeable chunks that have each with increments and values that should be the estimated cost of certain types of projects already. And as the increment part of the program needs to be understood with reference to when the United States should expect to see a return on the initial funding, recipient countries are prorated on those increments set for projects on a value rate that projects in all ways what essential additions can further be received through certain projects that other projects might follow. From America's standpoint, only by having set the program up in incremental project cost references in actuality of knowing how much each project would cost to create does it hedge against unvalued funding. The funding country benefits as well as the receiver nation.

Special Note

It has been my pleasure to provide you with a hard look into how America is allocating economy dollars for its own advancement as well as other nations. In this thesis/intelligence report I tried to bring to the forefront some of the information on what most would not readily have found by other sources and for that I take pride in this work. As it should relate to you the reader from the standpoint of an intelligence report, not all times do intelligence officers get to do this type of expose work. In being a part of an intelligence agency secrets are sometimes kept best untold. Also as an intelligence officer I am duty bound to work in the interest of national security and it has been deemed by those I serve that this report directly to the American people needed to be done. It will help you each live better informed and able to make intelligent decisions in your everyday lives. You will know what your country has stock in and how it directly affects your individual life. Again it has been my honor to provide you with this work and always remember that American intelligence agencies work for the interest of the American people and it should be no other way.